Mr. Greenleaf's Unforgettable Summer

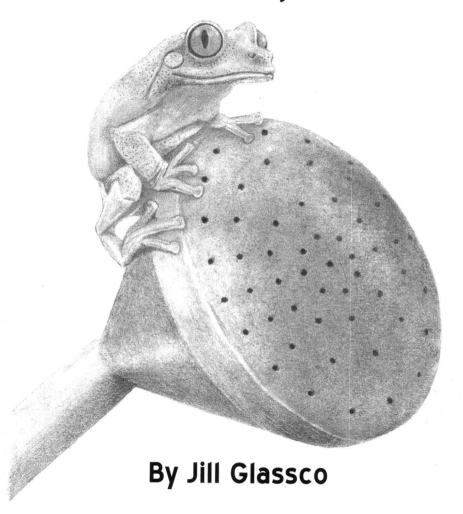

By Jill Glassco

Illustrated by:
Dawn Copeland

Copyright Page

ISBN-13: 978-1-939535-80-1

ISBN: 1939535808

www.deepseapublishing.com

Printed in the United States of America

Table of Contents

MR. GREENLEAF'S NOT-SO-TYPICAL DAY.. 5

BIG-BLUE MOUNTAIN..10

MOUNTAIN CLIMBING...14

MOUNTAINTOP VIEW...19

MRS. WILLOWKINS..24

MR. GREENLEAF'S CLOSE CALL..29

THE WEE-HUMANS..34

MR. GREENLEAF MEETS THE FAMILY..40

STORY TIME...46

MRS. WILLOWKINS TO THE RESCUE...51

GOOD NEWS..56

AFTERWORD...62

For my grandchildren:

Easton Jacob

Anya Elizabeth

Fisher Isaac

Colton Alexander

and

wee-grands yet to come

You are wondrous gifts from Jesus, and I love you so very, very much!

Memaw

"Grandchildren are the crowning glory of the aged..."
(Prov. 17:6a

Chapter 1
Mr. Greenleaf's Not-So-Typical Day

Mr. Greenleaf had lived beside the goldfish pond in Mrs. Willowkins' flower garden as long as he could remember – which wasn't very long since jumping and hopping, not recollecting, are a tree frog's strong suits. Hidden behind one stone south and two rocks west of the waterfall, his tiny cave provided shade from summer sun, shield from wind and rain, and shelter from winter's bitter cold.

"A pleasanter cottage a froggy is yet to find," J. Jehoshaphat Greenleaf estimated.

A typical "day" for Mr. Greenleaf began when the sun slid under Double Oak Mountain and stars sparkled over Blue Heron Lake, because tree frogs are strictly nocturnal, you see – sleeping in sunshine and hunting and leaping and singing and playing in the dark of the night. So our story begins once upon a summer sunset...

Twilight had faded to owllight, and the cricket choir sang a spirited tune to the beat of bullfrog bellows rising from the big lake below the Willowkins' small fishpond. Mr. Geenleaf opened his black peepers and slowly stretched his slim, lime legs.

Time for breakfast, he thought and then hopped through the small crevice to a narrow ledge above the pool. When a mosquito buz-z-z-z-z-zed by, out darted his long, sticky tongue; and breakfast was done.

Eyeing the silver marble peeking over the treetops, he spouted,

"Good evening, Mr. Man-in-the-Moon,

Shining bright upon navy blue.

Would you tell a froggy, please,

Now, what shall I do?"

Mr. Greenleaf cocked a teensy ear toward the sky and listened and listened and listened and waited and waited and waited. But Mr. Man-in-the-Moon just glared at the little frog with a frozen smile and didn't utter a word.

"Humph," said Mr. Greenleaf, "I shall search for another friend to guide me."

He studied the rocks with his protruding eyes and scanned the fishpond with his excellent binocular vision. Below the ivory pond lilies closed tight for the night, he spotted goldfish shimmering in the moonlight.

Mr. Greenleaf hopped closer to the water's edge and called down to the carp family,

"Excuse me, ladies and gentleman,

May I have your attention please?

Do you know a game to play

On water, rocks, or trees?"

One lone fishy glided to the surface, stuck her round mouth above the water, and noiselessly opened and closed, opened and closed her thin, orange lips. Mr. Greenleaf strained his neck toward the visitor and said, "What's that, madam? I can't hear one burble that you're saying."

Goldie simply winked a bubble eye at the amphibian, swirled around, and then returned to the other fish resting on the bottom of the pool. Mr. Greenleaf watched in bewilderment.

"My, my, quite curious,

Quite curious, I must say.

Maybe Cousin Kelly Greenleaf

Will want to hop and play."

A rustling in the woods, however, diverted his attention from fish and cousin. He pressed his little, green body against the rocks and sat exceedingly still - not twitching a muscle. For each evening, about this same point on the clock, Daniel Coon stopped by the fishpond on his way to who knows where. Because Mr. Greenleaf knew that little, green tree frogs sit at the top of a raccoon's list of favorite things to eat, he concentrated hard on not becoming Daniel's midnight snack.

But contrary to tradition, tonight the masked scavenger ignored the pond, scurried along the stone pathway toward the big house, and disappeared under the oak leaf hydrangeas. The frightened froggy sighed a great sigh of relief.

Feeling braver, Mr. Greenleaf jumped from the ledge into a pot of begonias beside the pond, took a deep breath, and called to his cousin in short, brassy honks. He honked seventy-five times in a mere minute, then paused and awaited her reply.

What happened next changed Mr. Greenleaf's typical day into not so typical whatsoever. Unexpectedly, a loud croak bellowed not from the big lake below the small fishpond, but only a few, short feet southeast of Mr. Greenleaf's begonia pot.

From her hiding place inside an old bird feeder Mrs. Willowkins had set on the garden floor, Cousin Kelly Greenleaf peeped as loud as her small voice would peep, "Jumping Jehoshaphat, leap for your life! Croaker, the bullfrog, has invaded our pond!"

Oh, my, my, my, what shall I do? Where shall I go? Mr. Greenleaf wondered in his wee, little mind. For you see, tree frogs understand from tadpolehood that bullfrogs, the largest frogs in

North America, have the severe reputation of being aggressive, opportunistic, ambush predators that eat any small animal they can stuff down their throats; and Joseph Caiaphas Croaker held the title of most voracious bullfrog in all of Shelby County.

Tree frogs in customary conditions easily startle, but poor Mr. Greenleaf grew terrified beyond horrified; and he started to cry.

"Doomed, good as dead,

And woe is me!

Somebody, help the frog.

Please, where should I be?"

At the end of his plea, a tiny light blinked on and off, on and off, on and off above the oak leaf hydrangea where Daniel, the raccoon, had vanished.

"It's a sign!" said Mr. Greenleaf hopefully. "Some kindhearted soul is guiding me."

Gathering every smidgen of courage he could muster, the little frog leaped from the pot onto the stone path, sprang toward the winking light as fast as his slim, lime legs would spring, and never looked back toward the tiny cave that had been his home as long as Jumping Jehoshaphat Greenleaf could remember.

REFLECTIONS
POINTS to PONDER

1. How did Mr. Greenleaf feel when Croaker invaded

   the pond? _____

2. When Croaker came to the fishpond, Mr. Greenleaf

   had to _____.

God's PROMISE to you:

"Don't be afraid, for I am with you. Don't be

discouraged, for I am your God. I will strengthen you

and help you. I will hold you up with My victorious

right hand."

(Isaiah 41:10 NLT)

(Hidden PEN POINT)

(**Joseph Caiaphas** was the Jewish high priest who

plotted to kill Jesus.)

(Read Matthew 26:3-4)

Can you find the hidden PEN POINT in chapter 2?

HINT: The hidden PEN POINT will always be

something from the Bible.

Chapter 2
Big-Blue Mountain

Sadly to say, before the froggy reached the signal, more lights blinked to the right of the stone path, to the left, under the oak leaf hydrangeas, and over.

Mr. Greenleaf's head drooped as he muttered, "Fireflies."

His pea-size heart sank lower than a snake's belly in a wagon rut. Feeling entirely befuddled, perplexed, and needless to say, extremely lonely and unhappy, the little tree frog crawled under an ivy leaf, closed his black eyes, and fell asleep a record two hours and thirty-seven minutes before daylight.

When he awoke the following evening, Mr. Man-in-the-Moon sat in his normal star-studded sky, and the cricket choir crooned their normal merry tune; but Mr. Greenleaf's circumstance didn't resemble normal by any stretch of the imagination – waking under an ivy leaf instead of snug in his tiny cave by the goldfish pond. He moaned,

"With tear-flooded cheeks,

I weep bitterly in the night.

For no one's here to comfort me

Or help to make things right."

Unbeknownst to Mr. Greenleaf, Barnabas Fieldmouse sat nearby nibbling sunflower seeds spilled from the new bird feeder Mr. Willowkins had hung by the screen porch and heard the pitiful lamentation.

"Hey now," said Barnabas, "what's all this blubbering about?"

Although some mice eat almost any kind of food findable, most are chiefly herbivores and favor seeds, berries, and grain over little, green tree frogs. Thus Mr. Greenleaf determined that this mouse most assuredly must be of the herb persuasion since he sounded so agreeable, so he crept from under the ivy to get a better look.

The old mouse had soft brown fur speckled with gray, stubby little legs, and a tail as long as his body. A field mouse's caution is sometimes mistaken for cowardly, but his carefulness had allowed ole Barnabas to live many a day in the crooks and crannies around the Willowkins' home place (making him an outstanding comrade-candidate for the discombobulated Mr. Greenleaf, I might add). His little, pink ears listened attentively to the homeless froggy's story of Croaker's take over.

Afterward, Mr. Fieldmouse rubbed his whiskers and said, "Chin up, my little friend. To think of how you outflanked that opportunist, Caiaphas Croaker, hornswoggled the hunter, and bamboozled that bullfrog, thoroughly boggles my miniature, mousy mind!"

"I did?" said Mr. Greenleaf.

"Certainly, you did, son," said Mr. Fieldmouse. "You're here, aren't you - alive and green as ever, young and strong with lots of hop left in those wiry, lime legs of yours."

"Come to think of it, I suppose I did make a monkey out of the ole bully - escaped right under his slimy nose, I did," said Mr. Greenleaf. He sat up a bit straighter and puffed out his little, tan chest.

"Why cry over yesterday's forfeitures, when you can press on toward tomorrow's possibilities?" said Mr. Fieldmouse. "What's stopping you from finding an even finer homestead than a tiny cave by a goldfish pond?"

By the time Mr. Fieldmouse concluded his salutation, Mr. Greenleaf's courage had grown two and a three-quarter sizes.

"I say, my good fellow," said Mr. Greenleaf, "not a single iota is preventing such a venture. Well, it was a pleasure meeting you, kind sir. I must be going now and hasten in my search for new shelter before sunrise. Adios, amigo!"

"Remember, lad," said Mr. Fieldmouse, "to a faithful friend, show yourself faithful, to a chum in need, show yourself accommodating, but to an ambush predator, always show yourself invisible; and life will go well with you. Adios, Greenleaf."

Mr. Greenleaf resumed his journey down the stone pathway - jumping right past the oak leaf hydrangeas, around the bend, and onto the slab below the Willowkins' screen porch. The concrete felt cool under his little, webbed feet, and he stopped to rest between two large urns of red geraniums and purple petunias.

Behind the urns, he discovered a large, chain-link kennel. It stood empty tonight; but sometimes two pooches - Gabe, an English Cream Golden Retriever, and Lucy, an Australian Shepherd – slept there when the children and grandchildren visited the Willowkins.

Regaining his wind, the froggy charged ahead in quest of new habitat. Reckoning that going right was right, he took a right hand turn past the right urn - leaping and jumping and hopping and bounding for mile after kilometer after mile in tree frog calculation, but essentially, 18.5 feet or 5.6387 meters in people calculation. The last leg of Mr. Greenleaf's trek brought him to the foot of an awe-inspiring, big, blue mountain – a 15-step staircase leading to the high deck beside the Willowkins' screen porch.

"I have frequently fancied what it would be like to live on a mountain," said Mr. Greenleaf. "What's stopping me from ascending this peak?"

At that moment, his tummy growled. Mr. Greenleaf hadn't eaten one bite since the mosquito buzzzzzed by the ledge of the fishpond over twenty-four hours prior, and all that hopping had made him enormously hungry.

Thankfully, a fresh mown lawn adjoined the sidewalk that adjoined Big-Blue Mountain, and Mr. Greenleaf heard a cricket twittering in the grass. He ever so quietly stalked the singing until his binocular peepers focused on the insect. Then out popped his sticky, pink tongue, and off hopped the froggy - fueled to the brim and ready for mountain climbing.

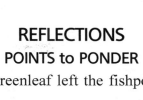

REFLECTIONS
POINTS to PONDER

1. When Mr. Greenleaf left the fishpond, he no longer had a _____.

2. Who encouraged Mr. Greenleaf? Mr. _____ Fieldmouse

God's PROMISE to you:

"Encourage each other. Live in harmony and peace. Then the God of love and peace will be with you." (2 Cor. 13:11b NLT)

(Hidden PEN POINT)

(**Barnabas** was the nickname for Joseph: an early Christian disciple from Cyprus who ministered with the apostle Paul. The name Barnabas means "son of encouragement.")

(Read Acts 4:36-37)

Can you find the hidden PEN POINT in chapter 3?

HINT: This time, it's a principle instead of a name.

Chapter 3
Mountain Climbing

Because little, green tree frogs have toe pads and long legs, they're excellent climbers as well as jumpers. His versatility, on the other hand, threw Mr. Greenleaf into a quandary – should he hop up the tall, blue steps or shimmy a spindle and climb the big mountain by way of the handrail?

The froggy thought and deliberated and pondered and considered and thought once more until his little, green head began to hurt. Mr. Greenleaf whined,

"This way or that way,

That way or this?

If that is the right way,

Is this way a miss?"

"What such," chattered a squeaky voice from high above Mr. Greenleaf's head.

Mr. Greenleaf jumped.

"Who... who's there?" said Mr. Greenleaf.

The stranger silently glided out of the darkness and landed as light as a feather on the ground beside the timid tree frog.

"Orville McNutt's the name," chattered the odd sort of animal. Thick, silky fur covered his smallish body – brown as a biscuit along his back and white as the driven snow on his belly.

14

Mr. Greenleaf stuttered,

"S –sir, pray tell,

Whatever you be.

Do you eat tree frogs?

Will you eat me?"

"What's the matter with you? Haven't you ever seen a flying squirrel before?" chattered Mr. McNutt. "Where were you born, sonny? Under a cabbage leaf?"

"Why no, indeed," said Mr. Greenleaf indignantly. "I'll have you know that I hatched in the goldfish pond of a particularly lovely *flower* garden planted just on the other side of Big-Blue Mountain."

"Well, everyone knows that Southern flying squirrels enjoy hickory nuts or acorns or seeds or mushrooms or maybe an insect or two from time to time, but never a leathery, little, beady-eyed, green tree frog," chattered Mr. McNutt. "So what's the problem, young man? You look as lost as a goose in a rainstorm."

"I wouldn't say that I'm lost, exactly," said Mr. Greenleaf. "I know where I was, and I know where I'm going. I just don't know which route to get me there."

"So where are you going?" chattered the squirrel.

"To the top of Big-Blue Mountain," said Mr. Greenleaf, "to find a new home."

"Then the one and only way to get there," chattered Mr. McNutt, "is by way of the stairs, because Daniel Coon staked claim to that handrail the first night he sneaked up the mountain and robbed Mrs. Willowkins' bird feeder."

"How do you know?" said Mr. Greenleaf.

"I know because I've visited the feeder a time or two myself – just to *borrow* a couple of seeds, mind you – and...." Suddenly Mr. McNutt stopped chattering.

"Quick!" he whispered. "Under the step. Here comes that rascal now."

Frog and squirrel scooted under the bottom step of Big-Blue Mountain just as Daniel, the raccoon, jumped off the handrail and waddled into the woods.

When the coast appeared clear, Mr. Greenleaf wailed, "Mercy me. Perhaps I best not ascend Big-Blue Mountain after all. Oh, now what shall I do? Mercy me, me, me."

"I think it best that you *do* make the climb," insisted Mr. McNutt. "Persevere, lad! Don't give up your dream of living on a mountaintop just because the journey's a tidbit harder than you anticipated. I happen to know that Mrs. Willowkins has pots and pots of flowers up there, one of which will make a dandy home for a green one such as yourself."

"Who is Mrs. Willowkins?" said Mr. Greenleaf.

"Oh, Mr. and Mrs. Willowkins are just a couple of harmless, old humans who take care of things around here like watering flowers, filling the feeders, and mowing the lawn," chattered Mr. McNutt. "Although they don't actually mow the grass themselves anymore since they found a younger, stronger he-human to do it for them."

"Oh," said Mr. Greenleaf.

"Daylight's just under the horizon, sonny. If you hurry your hopping, you can hop to the top of Big-Blue Mountain before dawn," chattered Mr. McNutt. "We night-timers need to get some shut-eye soon, so you better get a move on."

"But what about that renegade raccoon?" whimpered Mr. Greenleaf.

16

"Just show yourself invisible the 15 minutes he's visible and relish the mountain view the other 1,425 minutes of the day," chattered Mr. McNutt. "Well, I must be off. Cheerio, little chap!"

Before Mr. Greenleaf could ask another question, the flying squirrel scampered into the darkness, leaving the froggy all by his lonesome. Not knowing anything to do but follow the guidance of his newest friend, he adjusted his determination and declared,

"Charge up the staircase,

Onward, forward ho!

'Tis up to the mountain top

This frog shall surely go!"

Leaping onto step one in a single bound, Mr. Greenleaf subsequently conquered steps two, three, four; and not slowing down a bit, he bounded up two more. Step seven, step eight, steps nine and ten, he out jumped grasshoppers, fleas, mice, and men. Eleven, twwwwelve, thirrrrrrrteen, fooooourrrrteen, and seconds afore the dawn of twilight preceding sunrise, the little froggy sprang the last hurdle his slim, lime legs would spring and landed kerplop on the deck floor beside a watering pot. Too weary to explore any farther, the extremely tired, little tree frog crawled into the pot and fell fast asleep in the hollow of the handle.

REFLECTIONS
POINTS to PONDER

1. Why was Mr. Greenleaf afraid to climb Big-Blue Mountain? _____

    _____

2. Who encouraged Mr. Greenleaf to persevere and go after his dream even though the journey was harder than he thought? _____

    _____

God's PROMISE to you:

"So let's not get tired of doing what is good. At just the right time we will reap a harvest of blessing if we don't give up." (Gal. 6:9 NLT)

(Hidden PEN POINT)

(**Perseverance** is a biblical principle that means endurance, persistence, steadfastness, or not giving up in doing something despite difficulty or delays in achieving success.)

(Read Heb. 12:1-3)

Can you find the hidden PEN POINT in chapter 4?
HINT: It's a Bible verse.

Chapter 4
Mountaintop View

Mr. Greenleaf felt so exceptionally exhausted from his traumatic adventures and strenuous journey over the past two nights that Mr. Man-in-the-Moon rose and fell twice before the little fellow opened his black peepers again and found himself snug in the hollow of a watering pot handle instead of inside the tiny cave beside the goldfish pond. He inched through the handle and discovered just enough water in the bottom of the pot to quench his thirsty, pink tongue. On the outside of the plastic, olive green container, he stretched his slim, lime legs and investigated his new stomping grounds.

Beside the watering pot sat a large, cobalt blue planter overflowing with hot pink petunias, cotton candy begonias, and an Indian Sun daylily. Mr. Greenleaf noticed numerous flowerpots dotted over the deck like Orville McNutt had described; but it was the magnificent overhead scenery that captivated his undivided attention.

More twinkling stars than grains of sand on the seashore filled the night sky. At the fishpond, leafy branches of neighboring trees had limited Mr. Greenleaf's star gazing; therefore, tonight's heavens appeared as wide as the deep, blue ocean from this mountaintop view. Enthralled by the beauty, he sang,

"Such glory! Such splendor!

My feet want to dance!

My compliments to whomever

Made this expanse!"

The froggy hopped and twirled and leaped and spun and jumped and whirled until his little, green head became dizzy, but his pea-size heart grew quite merry indeed. Because a cheerful heart is good medicine, Mr. Greenleaf felt sunny on the inside and happier than a piggy in a mud puddle on the outside until a shadow moved across the dance floor.

As quiet as a church mouse, Daniel Coon had scaled the handrail, climbed onto the bird feeder, and there the ole boy sat helping himself to the black oil sunflower seeds, cracked corn, and safflower kernels that Mrs. Willowkins put out for her feathered friends. One second before panic, Mr. Greenleaf remembered Orville McNutt's advice: *just show yourself invisible the 15 minutes Mr. Coon is visible and relish the mountain view the other 1,425 minutes of the day.*

Consequently, Mr. Greenleaf hopped into a nearby pot of spearmint and blended into the fragrant foliage. Sure enough, after a

20

quarter turn of the minute hand, Daniel, the raccoon, jumped off the bird feeder to the handrail and crept down Big-Blue Mountain.

"Ahhhhhhhh, gone for the night," sighed Mr. Greenleaf in consolation, and he leaped from the mint onto the deck railing. "Now what?"

"Who," answered a soft, deep voice in the distance.

"No, not who - now *what*," insisted Mr. Greenleaf.

"Who, who," contended the voice again.

"I beg your pardon, sir, but I distinctly meant to say now *what* - meaning *what* shall I do now that Daniel Coon has departed the premises. I most certainly never intended to say now *who*," explained Mr. Greenleaf patiently.

"Who-who-ha-who," maintained the voice.

"I say, *who* goes there?" said Mr. Greenleaf. "Not that I'm agreeing, you understand. For I positively and clearly proposed 'now *what*' in my initial statement; but on secondary thought, *who,* may I ask, am I currently debating?"

"Who are you talking to, sonny?" chattered a familiar voice from the top of Mrs. Willowkins' bird feeder.

"Mr. McNutt!" said Mr. Greenleaf. "How wonderful to see you again, my good man. I followed your wise recommendation and made myself

21

invisible when Daniel Coon made his nightly rounds, and then simply asked the fundamental question 'now what?' Subsequently, some argumentative creature voiced his dispute, and continues to do so, by saying, 'who-who-ha-who,' when I deliberately stated now what *not* who!"

"Greenleaf, you're too gullible for your own good," chattered Mr. McNutt. "It's a trap. The only whoer 'round these parts is Sir Solomon – a Great Horned Owl of North America and fierce hunter that lives on the other side of Blue Heron Lake. He hides in the dense tree cover and then sits patiently to hear the tiniest pipe from any animal such as a rabbit or a little, green tree frog that, with one fell swoop, makes a dainty morsel for his who-ha-who mouth. Caiaphas Croaker and Daniel Coon pale in comparison to this powerful predator. I hear tell that once ole Solomon heard a mouse squeak from 900 feet away; and not only that, his sharp vision in low light enables him to see what's in front of those intimidating, yellow eyes as well as behind by turning his head over halfway around. Sonny, when you hear Solomon's who-who-ha-who, immediately make yourself invisible *and* silent. Comprendo?"

Mr. Greenleaf gulped and nodded his little, green head. "So many enemies of little, green tree frogs," lamented Mr. Greenleaf. "What's a froggy to do?"

"Simply make yourself invisible when Mr. Coon is visible, make yourself invisible *and* silent when Solomon is audible, and enjoy the mountain view all the other tick tocks of the clock," chattered Mr. McNutt. "Well, cheerio, little chap."

The flying squirrel leaped from the feeder and sailed into the night, leaving Mr. Greenleaf very much alone again. The disheartened froggy sighed. A big dose of merry-heart medicine would have done him a world of good at that moment; but tonight, that pill seemed too big to swallow for the timid, little tree frog that had fixed his black peepers on his problems rather than his blessings.

Without so much as a flea for supper, he crept into the watering pot, wriggled into the hollow of the handle, and drifted off to sleep. Hours later, in the heat of the day, a sudden jolt woke Mr. Greenleaf. The watering pot was moving!

REFLECTIONS
POINTS to PONDER

1. What did Mr. Greenleaf see that made his heart merry
    and his feet dance?

    _____

    _____

2. Mr. Greenleaf lost his cheerful heart because he
    focused on his problems rather than his

    _____.

God's PROMISE to you:

*Jesus said, "I am leaving you a gift – peace of mind and
heart. And the peace I give is a gift the world cannot give.
So don't be troubled or afraid." (John 14:27 NLT)*

(Hidden PEN POINT)

(Bible verse: ***A cheerful heart is good medicine***, *but a
broken spirit saps a person's strength." Proverbs 17:22
NLT*)

Can you find the hidden PEN POINT in chapter 5?

Chapter 5
Mrs. Willowkins

Mr. and Mrs. Pickleheimer, the original caretakers of the big house over Blue Heron Lake, passed the overseer-baton into the hands of Mr. and Mrs. Willowkins only a few years before Mr. Greenleaf hatched in the goldfish pond. Having raised three little Willowkins in a small cottage in North Shelby County, some feared the Willowkins were afflicted with a severe case of mid-life crisis when the empty nesters upsized their stewardship duties rather than downsized.

Mrs. Willowkins just smiled – something Mrs. Willowkins is known to do regularly – and said, "Don't worry, dearies. We're just stretching our tent, lengthening our cords, and strengthening our stakes to make room for the next generation of wee Willowkins."

Martha Willowkins was an odd sort of she-human that seemed to always be in a hurry even when there was no place to hurry to or no reason to hurry for. She scurried around the kitchen, jogged down the aisles at the grocery store, and darted across the yard while watering her pots and pots and more pots of petunias, begonias, periwinkles, and geraniums. Oftentimes, Mr. Willowkins shook his head and chuckled as he watched his bride of practically forty years bustle from one thingamajig to another like a honeybee from blossom to blossom.

All that to say, as you may have already guessed, Mrs. Willowkins (not knowing that a little, green tree frog had taken up residence in her watering pot) had picked up the container, carried it inside the house to the sink in her pink and green laundry room, and started filling it with water.

An earthquake! A flood! feared Mr. Greenleaf. *What shall I do? Where shall I go?*

As water engulfed the pot handle, he edged backwards until he circled out the other end and fell into the flooded belly. With the container nearing overflow, out of the watering pot hopped Mr. Greenleaf, and out of the startled Mrs. Willowkins popped a piercing shriek. Because the shrill noise profoundly alarmed the little, green tree frog that had never seen a she-human before, he jumped about the sink desperately trying to find a hiding place from this strange, hysterical creature. When her squeals changed to giggles, however, Mr. Greenleaf returned to the side of the pot; and Mrs. Willowkins carted froggy and lodge outside to the deck where he exited the pot and hid in a tight space between the cobalt blue planter and the screen porch.

(The too-frightened froggy had failed to properly introduce himself, so Mrs. Willowkins had no earthly notion of Jumping Jehoshaphat Greenleaf's given name. Therefore, she addressed the tree frog, ever so sweetly, as *Mr. Green Jeans*.)

"It's okay, Mr. Green Jeans. I won't hurt you," she said and then walked inside the big house over Blue Heron Lake.

Mr. Greenleaf sat perfectly still and stared through the screen. He couldn't believe his peepers. On the other side of the wire, under a maidenhair fern, a small turtle also stood motionless – not twitching a muscle just like Mr. Greenleaf.

"I think the she-human is gone," whispered Mr. Greenleaf.

The turtle neither moved nor spoke.

"I say, madam, I do believe the coast is clear," said Mr. Greenleaf. "How long have you been standing there as still as a stone statue, my friend?"

But the turtle didn't answer or even so much as blink a glassy eye.

"On second glance, madam, I believe you *are* a statue," said Mr. Greenleaf. "Nonetheless, you shall be my friend – my stone turtle statue friend named...uh...uh...I have it! You shall be my little, turtle friend named Fern."

Mr. Greenleaf yawned. "Well, I must be going now, Fern. I'm normally a night-timer, you know; so perhaps I'll visit you again when Mr.

Man-in-the-Moon shines over Blue Heron Lake and the cricket choir croons their merry tune. Good day, my new friend," said the froggy, and then he bounced into the watering pot, squirmed up the handle, and once more fell fast asleep.

When Mr. Willowkins came home for lunch, Mrs. Willowkins said, "Wilbur, you'll never guess what hopped out of my watering pot this morning."

But before Mr. Willowkins had time to guess, Mrs. Willowkins answered for him. "A tree frog! When that froggy jumped in my face, I squawked like a barnyard hen and scared the poor, little thing nigh to expiration. He jumped loops around the sink until finally hopping back on the watering pot, and then I promptly carried him outside. I named the cute, little critter Mr. Green Jeans. Guess where I got that name, Wilbur."

Mr. Willowkins had opened his mouth to answer when Mrs. Willowkins spouted, "Captain Kangaroo! Remember Mr. Green Jeans, Dancing Bear, and Grandfather Clock? I loved that show as a kid in the 60s. Didn't you, dear?"

Mr. Willowkins just nodded and grinned and then held up an envelope. "A letter from the grandchildren came today."

Mrs. Willowkins' brown eyes sparkled like Christmas tree lights, and she clapped both hands together. "A letter from the grandchildren. How wonderful! What did they say?"

"They're coming for a visit next week," said Mr. Willowkins.

"Next week! Oh, wonderful, simply wonderful," said Mrs. Willowkins excitedly. "I'll need to get their beds ready and clean the screen porch – you know how those children love to play on the screen porch – and make a grocery list of their favorite foods."

Sidetracked from fixing lunch for Mr. Willowkins, Mrs. Willowkins dashed to her desk to grab a pen and then zipped across the kitchen to snatch the grocery-list pad stuck to the refrigerator. Smiling, Mr. Willowkins finished the tuna salad Mrs. Willowkins had started but long since forgotten.

REFLECTIONS
POINTS to PONDER

1. Who moved Mr. Greenleaf's watering pot?

   _____

2. Martha Willowkins is always in a _____

   even when there's no reason to rush.

God's PROMISE to you:

"God is our refuge and strength, always ready to help

in times of trouble...

Be still and know that I am God." (Psalm 46:1,10 NLT)

(Hidden PEN POINT)

(**Martha**, Mary, and Lazarus were siblings and Jesus'
special friends. Martha was known for her busyness in
serving meals and caring for houseguests;

while her sister, Mary, was known for sitting at Jesus'
feet and listening.)

(Read Luke 10:38-42)

Can you find the hidden PEN POINT in chapter 6?

Chapter 6
Mr. Greenleaf's Close Call

When twilight faded to dusk, Mr. Greenleaf opened his black peepers and heard the pitter-patter of raindrops bouncing from the handle of the watering pot. Thunder boomed in the distance trailed by flashes of lightening across the night sky, and Mr. Man-in-the-Moon played hide and seek behind the heavy, rolling clouds.

Whereas human creatures run to shelter in rainstorms, froggys, on the other hand, frolic in the droplets that moisten their thirsty, green skin. Eager to splash and play, Mr. Greenleaf hurried out of the hollow handle.

"How invigorating," said Mr. Greenleaf, and he began to sing,

"I love a rainy,

Starless night –

A sky that rumbles

And flashes light."

Mr. Greenleaf sang at the top of his little froggy lungs and jumped from puddle to puddle around and around the Willowkins' deck. Three-fourths about his third circle, however, Mr. Greenleaf came face to face with the crafty Daniel Coon. In his rain-shower ecstasy, the little tree frog had completely disremembered making himself invisible the 15 minutes the raccoon was visible atop Big-Blue Mountain.

"Well, hello there, my little, green friend," said Mr. Coon, eyeing Mr. Greenleaf with a sly grin. "How good it is to see you this evening."

Since Mrs. Willowkins made a habit of not filling the bird feeder on rainy nights, Daniel, the raccoon, had missed his regular black oil sunflower seed and cracked corn supper; thus, this evening, the little, green tree frog looked especially appetizing to the ambush predator.

Mr. Greenleaf stared at the marauder in wide-eyed silence.

"My, what slim, lime legs you have," said Mr. Coon, creeping slowly toward his target. "Let me get a better look at those fine specimens."

Just when Mr. Greenleaf numbered himself a goner for sure, Mrs. Willowkins switched on the floodlight and stepped onto the screen porch.

"Look, Wilbur," called Mrs. Willowkins. "That pesky raccoon is back – trying to empty the bird feeder again, no doubt. Shoo Mr. Raccoon. Go find your supper on Blue Heron Lake."

Wasting no time, Mr. Coon swiftly scrambled down Big-Blue Mountain, this time by way of the 15-step staircase, and vanished into the woods.

Mrs. Willowkins opened the screen door. "Why Mr. Green Jeans," she said. "Why are you visible while that raiding raccoon is visible? Next time he's around, hide in your watering pot where you'll be safe and sound."

Mr. Greenleaf gratefully blinked his black peepers at the she-human, puffed out his throat, and croaked, "Thank you ever so kindly, madam," which sounded like a honk to Mrs. Willowkins since she speaks only English and not Froggish. She laughed and walked back inside to Mr. Willowkins. Immediately, the froggy leaped toward the cobalt blue planter, slipped behind the pot, and peered through the screen wire at his new friend.

"I say, Fern, did you see what just happened?" said Mr. Greenleaf. "If it weren't for Mrs. Willowkins' defense, unquestionably, I would have breathed my last – bit the dust – kicked the bucket – been pushing up daisies for certain!"

Fern stood stone still.

"That kindhearted she-human saved my life. Good heavens, she can call me Mr. Green Jeans or Puddin' Tame, for that matter, just as long as she calls me out of the clutches of that cunning Mr. Coon. This date is truly noteworthy indeed, for I have made two faithful friends – Fern, my little, statue turtle friend and Martha Willowkins, my first ever in my entire history she-human friend. A wise one once said that a real friend sticks closer than a brother, and I now have two real friends."

The rain slowed to a drizzle, and Mr. Greenleaf returned to splashing from puddle to puddle and singing,

"Ole Daniel Coon came a huntin'

On Big-Blue Mountaintop.

When he aimed for Jumping Jehoshaphat,

Mrs. Willowkins made him stop!"

As nights passed, Mr. Greenleaf discovered that from the tip top of his watering pot spout and the outside window stools along the deck of the big house over Blue Heron Lake, he had a grand view of the Willowkins' screen porch, kitchen, and living room. Because he found people watching quite engaging, he longed less and less for the good old days at the goldfish pond.

Each evening, the moment that twilight dimmed to dusk, Mr. Greenleaf opened his black peepers, stretched his slim, lime legs, wiggled through the hollow of the handle, and hopped out of the watering pot to see what he could see.

"I do say, Fern, those humans have the strangest ways," said Mr. Greenleaf on the night before the wee-humans arrived. "Tonight, Mrs. Willowkins combined and mixed and stirred and then poured a concoction that looked something akin to Mississippi mud into a metal pot. She proceeded to place that pot in a red-hot box, hotter than the noonday sun; and an hour later, she turned the brown brick onto a glass circle. I find that odd, don't you?"

Mr. Greenleaf hopped to the very tip of the watering pot spout, and called down to his turtle friend, "Fern, you won't believe what's happening now. Mr. Willowkins just cut the brick with a knife and is eating it!"

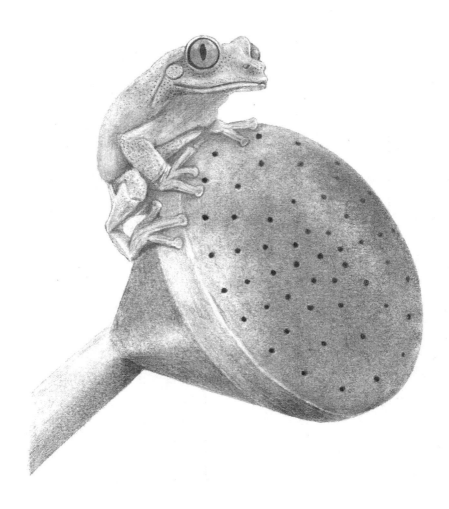

"Martha, this is the best cake you've ever made," said Mr. Willowkins.

"Save some for the children, dear," said Mrs. Willowkins. "You know Jacob loves my sour cream, chocolate chip pound cake."

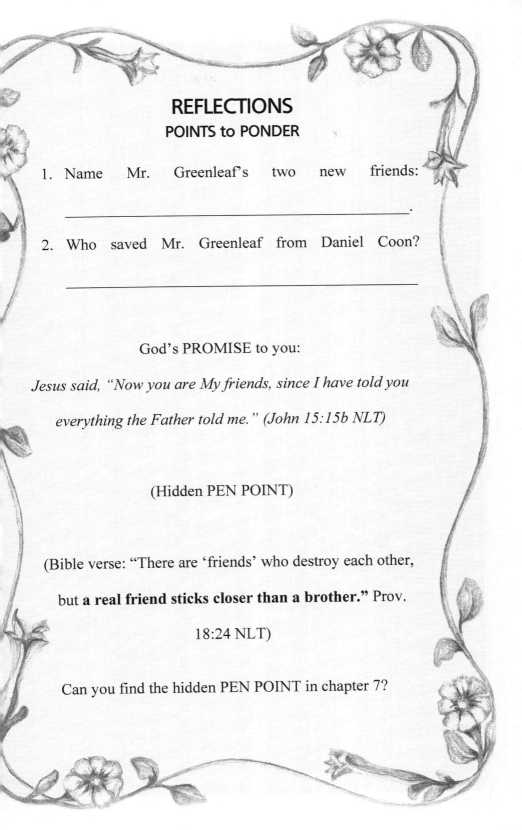

REFLECTIONS
POINTS to PONDER

1. Name Mr. Greenleaf's two new friends:

_____.

2. Who saved Mr. Greenleaf from Daniel Coon?

_____

God's PROMISE to you:

Jesus said, "Now you are My friends, since I have told you

everything the Father told me." (John 15:15b NLT)

(Hidden PEN POINT)

(Bible verse: "There are 'friends' who destroy each other,

but **a real friend sticks closer than a brother."** Prov.

18:24 NLT)

Can you find the hidden PEN POINT in chapter 7?

Chapter 7
The Wee-humans

Mr. Greenleaf was sleeping peacefully in the hollow handle of the watering pot when the wee-humans arrived. Mrs. Willowkins' nose had been pressed against the library windowpane for over an hour while watching for the gray minivan, which finally turned onto the driveway.

"Wilbur, they're here!" she called happily.

Mr. and Mrs. Willowkins hurried outside to greet their children, grandchildren, and granddog, Lucy, already piling out of the car. After hugs and kisses and more hugs and kisses, Mrs. Willowkins exclaimed, "Wilbur, can you believe how tall Jacob has grown? Jacob, you'll be taller than Mamaw soon. And Elizabeth, you get prettier everyday, just like your mama. Isaac, let me feel those muscles."

Instantly, Isaac made fists and raised both arms to show off his superhero muscles. "Strongest five-year-old I've ever seen," said Mrs. Willowkins proudly.

"When is baby Alexander coming?" said Jacob.

"Oh, everyone will be here for supper, dear," said Mrs. Willowkins, "both aunts, both uncles, your sweet baby cousin, and of course doggie cousin, Gabe. You won't believe how big baby Alexander is – growing like a weed just like the three of you. Come on in the house now. I have little surprises for you children. Can you guess what they are?"

"Legos?" said Jacob.

"A stuffed animal?" said Elizabeth.

"Little cars?" said Isaac.

"How did you ever guess?" said Mrs. Willowkins.

The children just smiled at one another knowing that their grandmother had the same "surprises" every visit.

That evening, singing voices woke Mr. Greenleaf two and a quarter hours before the sun slid behind Double Oak Mountain.

"The Lord is good to me,

And so I thank the Lord,

For giving me

The things I need -

The sun, and the rain, and the apple seed.

The Lord is good to me.

Amen!"

What a lovely melody. I wonder who's singing, thought Mr. Greenleaf, *and who is the Lord?*

Uncertain as to whether he should be visible or invisible, the little tree frog stretched his slim, lime legs, quietly crept to the opening of the watering pot, and peeped through the window into the Willowkins' tremendously full kitchen. Humans were everywhere – he-humans, she-humans, wee-humans, and one teeny-human – an even dozen to be exact.

Mrs. Willowkins never looked merrier. She wore a smile that stretched from ear to ear as she flitted from human to human like a happy hummingbird in a beautiful rose garden. The open door between the screen porch and kitchen allowed Mr. Greenleaf to eavesdrop on the family's conversation.

"Elizabeth, would you like more macaroni and cheese?" said Mrs. Willowkins.

"What's for dessert?" said Jacob.

"You need to eat your supper before we talk about dessert," said his mother.

"Chocolate chip pound cake," whispered Mrs. Willowkins in Jacob's ear.

"Mamaw, did you get some gummies for me?" said Isaac.

"Eat your supper first," said his mother sweetly.

Mrs. Willowkins winked at Isaac and nodded.

"Da, da, da, da, da," said baby Alexander, and everyone laughed.

After supper, all twelve humans crowded onto the screen porch. Twinkling stars glittered the night sky, and Mr. Man-in-the-Moon's reflection danced across Blue Heron Lake to the cricket choirs' joyful tune.

"Mamaw, will you tell us a story?" said Isaac.

"Tell us a Bible story,' said Elizabeth.

Baby Alexander sat in Mrs. Willowkins lap and smiled at Jacob making funny faces.

"Let me see," said Mrs. Willowkins. "Well, children, did you know that a long, long, long time ago there was no Mr. Man-in-the-Moon, no shiny stars, humans, or even little, green tree frogs?"

Mr. Greenleaf gasped.

"Did y'all hear something?" said Mr. Willowkins.

Disregarding his question, Mrs.

Willowkins continued the creation story. "The Lord God tells us in Genesis..."

The Lord? thought Mr. Greenleaf. *He's the one in that delightful song, and He's God!*

"...that in the beginning, He made the heavens and the earth, but the earth spun empty and dark – black as soot and darker than a moonless night."

"Woe, that's dark," said Isaac.

"Then the Lord God said, 'Let there be light' and there was light. And the light was good because God is so good and such a wondrous Creator," said Mrs. Willowkins. "So good, that each time He spoke, it happened quicker than you can say Wilbur Willowkins wore a winter weskit."

Mr. Willowkins winked, and the children giggled.

"God told waters to gather in one place, and kaboom, there were oceans. He told the earth to sprout, and tada, there were ferns and fruit trees and all kinds of seed-bearing plants. He spoke the sun and the moon and the stars into the heavens, and water creatures into the oceans, land creatures onto solid ground, and birds of every kind into the air."

"I'm a land creature!" croaked Mr. Greenleaf enthusiastically.

"What is that sound?" demanded Mr. Willowkins.

"Then, last but not least, God said, 'Let's make special creatures in Our image, according to Our likeness; and let them rule over the fish of the sea and over all the other creatures of the earth.' And in that instant, God made a man and named him Adam," said Mrs. Willowkins.

"Why did God say "Our" image?" said Elizabeth.

"Good question, Elizabeth," said Mr. Willowkins. "It's because our God is Three in One."

"Huh?" said Elizabeth.

"Think of it this way. Remember from your science lesson that one hydrogen atom, and another hydrogen atom, and an oxygen atom *together* make a water molecule?" said Mr. Willowkins.

"Yes, sir," said Elizabeth.

"Well, the heavenly Father, His Son, and the Holy Spirit *together* make God," said Mr. Willowkins.

"Amazing!" honked Mr. Greenleaf.

"Papaw, I heard something, too," said Isaac.

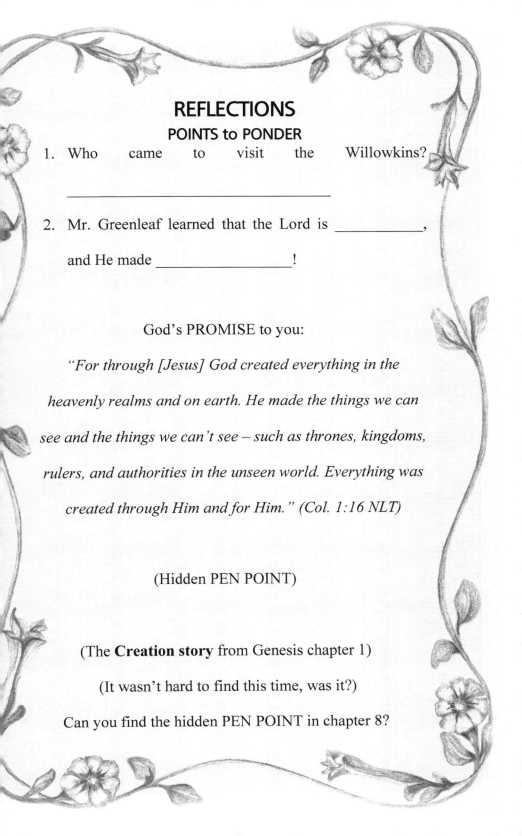

REFLECTIONS
POINTS to PONDER

1. Who came to visit the Willowkins?

   _____

2. Mr. Greenleaf learned that the Lord is _____,

   and He made _____!

God's PROMISE to you:

"For through [Jesus] God created everything in the

heavenly realms and on earth. He made the things we can

see and the things we can't see – such as thrones, kingdoms,

rulers, and authorities in the unseen world. Everything was

created through Him and for Him." (Col. 1:16 NLT)

(Hidden PEN POINT)

(The **Creation story** from Genesis chapter 1)

(It wasn't hard to find this time, was it?)

Can you find the hidden PEN POINT in chapter 8?

Chapter 8
Mr. Greenleaf Meets the Family

The Lord is God, and He made everything – even little, green tree frogs, marveled Mr. Greenleaf. *That means the Lord God made me! I can't wait to tell Fern.*

Mr. Greenleaf could hardly contain himself to remain invisible until the he, she, wee, and teeny humans left the porch and turned in for the night. As soon as the kitchen light switched off, the tree frog bounded from the watering pot and called through the wire screen to his little, stone friend, "My dear, Fern, did you hear Mrs. Willowkins' Bible story? Did you ever in your life fathom that the Lord is God and He made *everything?*"

"What's that you're saying?" chattered a squeaky voice.

Mr. Greenleaf jumped. *"Fern?"*

"Where are you, sonny," chattered Orville McNutt.

"Oh, here I am, Mr. McNutt," said Mr. Greenleaf, and he hopped from behind the cobalt blue planter. "And I have marvelous news to share...

The Lord is *God*, and

He made Mr. Man-in-the-Moon,

All the shining stars, and

Even Daniel, the raccoon."

"You don't say," said Mr. McNutt.

"I do say," said Mr. Greenleaf. "And the humans sing songs to Him before eating macaroni and cheese. Oh, I do hope Mrs. Willowkins tells the wee-humans another Bible story tomorrow night on the screen porch."

"Wee-humans? Wee-humans you say?" chattered Mr. McNutt. "You best make yourself invisible when wee-humans come around. You can't judge a book by it's cover, sonny. Why, those miniatures may appear as innocent as newborn lambs on the outside, but you just never know what those wee-ones might do to a little, green tree frog. You just neeeever know!"

Mr. Greenleaf swallowed anxiously. His happy face wilted, and his cheerfulness shrank a half size as worry wiggled into his wee, little mind.

"Oh, my," said Mr. Greenleaf. "Yes, I'll be especially cautious while the wee-humans visit the Willowkins. Thank you, Mr. McNutt."

The following day, Mr. Greenleaf snoozed soundly in the hollow handle of the watering pot, not budging an inch when Mrs. Willowkins picked it up and peered inside.

"I don't think Mr. Green Jeans is here today, children," she said and once again carried the pot inside the big house and filled it with water.

Startled from the deep sleep, Mr. Greenleaf shook his little, green head to clear his thoughts and then felt cool water tickling his little, webbed toes.

"Mrs. Willowkins, I'm here!" he babbled, but she didn't seem to hear.

"Oh, dear me, me, me, me! What shall I do?" cried Mr. Greenleaf. "Think, think, think!"

41

But there was no time for thinking because the water rose rapidly through the handle. Although tree frogs can comfortably remain underwater for a rather long time, being submerged within the narrow confines of the watering pot handle made Mr. Greenleaf severely nervous. Hence the amphibian swam out of his hiding place; and then with one giant jump, he shot from the watering pot like a musket ball from a muzzle-loaded rifle and belly flopped onto the Willowkins' hardwood floor.

Mrs. Willowkins exclaimed, "Jacob! Elizabeth! Isaac! Come quickly! It's Mr. Green Jeans!"

"Wee-humans!" honked Mr. Greenleaf.

Mr. McNutt's warning rang like clanging symbols in his little, green ears: "Make yourself invisible when wee-humans come around. You just never know what they'll do to a little, green tree frog. Make yourself invisible."

Make myself invisible; make myself invisible, thought Mr. Greenleaf, as he hopped around the kitchen.

"Catch him, Jacob!" said Mrs. Willowkins.

Jacob lunged for the tree frog and caught him in a loose fist. But quick as a flash, Mr. Greenleaf vaulted out of the hole between Jacob's thumb and forefinger, and the race was on. Mr. Greenleaf jumped, Jacob chased, Elizabeth squealed, Isaac giggled, Mrs. Willowkins shouted, "Catch him, Jacob. Catch him!" and Mr. Willowkins and the two adult-child-humans just sat back and watched the circus.

After a lap around the kitchen table, Jacob finally hemmed Mr. Greenleaf into a corner. Getting on his hands and knees, he looked kindly into the froggy's beady, black eyes, and said, "It's okay, Mr. Green Jeans. I won't hurt you. I'm just trying to help you get back home."

Although Mr. Greenleaf's heart pounded one hundred and two miles an hour, he sat perfectly still, allowing Jacob to pick him up and carry him outside. The boy gently petted the little, green back while Mrs. Willowkins watered her flowers, and then he carefully placed the froggy on the side of the empty pot.

"See Mr. Green Jeans; you're okay. Everything's just fine now," said Jacob.

"Good job, Jacob," said Mrs. Willowkins. "Climb in your watering pot, Mr. Green Jeans, and go back to sleep. I'm sorry we disturbed your nap. Come on Jacob; let's go eat lunch."

After the she and wee-human disappeared, Mr. Greenleaf clambered into the watering pot and cuddled up in the hollow handle.

These wee-Willowkins differ entirely from the wee-humans Mr. McNutt described, pondered Mr. Greenleaf. *I wonder if that squirrely rodent's ever even met a wee-human, or if he formulated his bad estimation purely by tittle-tattle? I believe Jacob, Elizabeth, and Isaac are my true friends, as true as Mrs. Willowkins, and certainly not ambush predators.*

The froggy yawned; and just before drifting into dreamland, Mr. Greenleaf recited Mr. Fieldmouse's noble advice. "To a faithful friend, show yourself faithful, to a chum in need, show yourself accommodating, but to an ambush predator, always show yourself invisible; and life will go well with you."

REFLECTIONS

POINTS to PONDER

1. Mr. McNutt warned Mr. Greenleaf not to trust

_____.

2. Should you judge others by someone else's opinion?

YES   NO

God's PROMISE to you:

"Do not judge others, and you will not be judged. For you will

be treated as you treat others. The standard you use in judging is

the standard by which you will be judged." (Matt. 7:1-2 NLT)

(Hidden PEN POINTs)

(**Jacob** – son of Isaac and Rebekah, twin brother of Esau, renamed "Israel" by God, and the father of 12 sons – patriarchs of the 12 tribes of Israel. See Gen. 25 and 35.)

(**Elizabeth** – wife of Zacharias, cousin of Mary (Jesus' mother), and the mother of John the Baptist. See Luke 1)

(**_Isaac_** – God's promised son to Abraham and Sarah, husband of Rebekah, and the father of Jacob and Esau. See Gen. 21, 24, and 25.)

Can you find the hidden PEN POINT in chapter 9?

Chapter 9
Story Time

Do you know that electrified, overjoyed, excited feeling you have when you wake up on the morning of your birthday or Christmas Day or the first day of summer vacation? Well, that's precisely how Mr. Greenleaf felt when he woke up later that same summer day and heard he, she, wee, and teeny-Willowkins' voices on the screen porch.

"Mamaw, it's time for another Bible story," said Elizabeth.

Mr. Greenleaf's teensy ears perked up as tall as a little, green tree frog's ears can perk. He wiggled down the handle and perched on the watering pot spout so as not to miss a single word.

Splendid, thought the froggy, *another Bible story!*

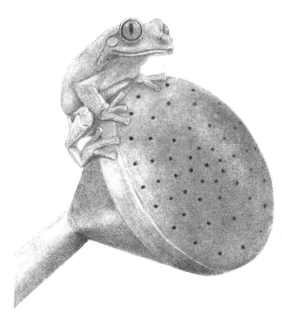

"Have I ever told you about the forty year camping trip?" said Mrs. Willowkins.

"I wanna go camping," said Isaac.

"Not for forty years!" said Elizabeth.

"Papaw, did someone really camp out for forty years," said Jacob, "or is Mamaw just pulling our leg?"

"It's true. A camping trip through the desert that should have taken only eleven days turned into a forty-year journey in the wilderness for Moses and the children of Israel," said Mr. Willowkins.

"How come?" said Elizabeth.

"Well, God's children, the Israelites, had lived in Egypt for a long time - Exodus 12:40 says 430 years," said Mrs. Willowkins. "And even though the Lord loved His people greatly, they had become slaves to the Egyptians."

"When something bad happens, it doesn't means that God doesn't love us," added Mr. Willowkins. "And when we sin, or do something wrong, God still loves us, just like your parents still love you even when you make mistakes."

"That's good because I make a lot of mistakes," said Jacob.

"Me, too," said Mr. Willowkins.

"Well, the Israelites cried and cried to God for help," said Mrs. Willowkins, "and at His appointed time, the Lord sent a deliverer named Moses. After Moses' persistent petitions and God's 10 formidable miracles, Pharaoh finally let God's people go. But no sooner had the dust settled from millions of marching feet leaving Goshen, than the evil ruler changed his mind and chased after the Israelites all the way to the Red Sea."

Flabbergasted, Mr. Greenleaf edged to the tiptop of his spout.

"Mighty soldiers, horses, and chariots closed in behind God's children, and crashing waves of the sea stretched out before them; but Moses said, 'Don't be afraid! Just stand still and watch the Lord rescue you today. He'll fight for you Himself! Just stay calm.' Then the Lord said to Moses, 'Tell the people to get moving! Moses, you pick up your staff and raise your hand over the Red Sea, and I'll split the waters so My children can walk through the middle on dry ground.' Then the angel of the Lord leading the people moved to the rear of the camp along with a pillar of cloud, which stood between the Egyptians and Israelites; and as darkness fell, the cloud turned to fire!"

"Wow!" croaked Mr. Greenleaf.

"Isaac, did you burp?" said his mother. "Say, excuse me, please."

"Wasn't me!" insisted Isaac.

Mrs. Willowkins gave a questioning glance toward her watering pot on the high deck and then resumed the story. "So Moses raised his staff, and with a strong east wind, the Lord opened a path through the water. The people marched right through the middle of the sea on dry ground, with high walls of water on each side. The Egyptians came after them. But when the sun began to rise, Moses raised his staff again, and the Lord closed the sea - sweeping the enemy soldiers and chariots away."

"It's almost bedtime, " said the pretty adult-child-human. "Mamaw may have to finish this story tomorrow."

"Just a few more minutes," begged the wee-humans. "Pleeeeeease, Mama!!!"

"Okay," she said, "just ten more minutes."

"I'll hurry," said Mrs. Willowkins. "Well, God vowed to take His children to a wonderful Promise Land – the land of Canaan, and He told Moses to send 12 spies to inspect the place God had promised. After 40 days, the spies returned and described a bountiful land flowing with milk and honey; however, powerful people, fortified cities, and even giants occupied Canaan. Two of the spies, Caleb and Joshua, believed God's promise and said, 'Let's go take the land,' but the other ten spies and the multitude of people had great fear instead of faith in God. They grumbled and complained and were afraid to take the Promise Land; so the Lord disciplined their unfaithfulness by turning the 11-day trip into a 40-year journey around and around and around the desert. During all those 40 years, however, the Lord loved His children. He provided food for them and guided them with a cloud by day and a pillar of fire by night. Psalm 48:14 tells us 'that is what God is like. He is our God forever and ever, and He will guide us until we die.'"

Mr. Willowkins said, "The Lord still guides and takes care of His creatures."

"Even me?" said Elizabeth.

"Of course you," said Mr. Willowkins.

"Even Mr. Green Jeans?" said Jacob.

"Even Mr. Green Jeans," said Mrs. Willowkins. "The Lord said in Matthew chapter 6, 'Just look at the birds. They don't plant or harvest or store food in barns, for your heavenly Father feeds them.'"

"We feed the birds at our house," said Isaac.

"I'm so glad you do, dear," said Mrs. Willowkins. "God feeds His feathered friends through your precious, little hands. Did you know that whenever someone helps you know the good way to go or the right thing

to do, it's really the Lord guiding you? Well, it's bedtime, children. Elizabeth, would you like to talk to God tonight?"

"Sure," said Elizabeth.

Next, all the he, she, and wee-humans bowed their heads and closed their eyes, so Mr. Greenleaf did, too.

"Dear God," said Elizabeth, "thank You for letting us come to Alabama to visit Papaw and Mamaw Willowkins. Thank You for guiding us and taking care of us and for taking care of all the animals. Thank You for our new friend, Mr. Green Jeans, and please keep him safe. Amen."

"Amen," said the Willowkins family.

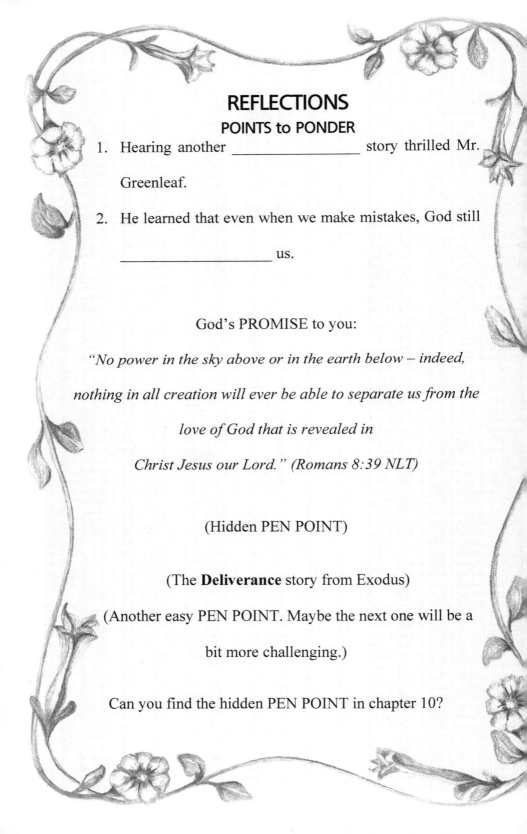

REFLECTIONS
POINTS to PONDER

1. Hearing another _____ story thrilled Mr. Greenleaf.

2. He learned that even when we make mistakes, God still _____ us.

God's PROMISE to you:

"No power in the sky above or in the earth below – indeed,

nothing in all creation will ever be able to separate us from the

love of God that is revealed in

Christ Jesus our Lord." (Romans 8:39 NLT)

(Hidden PEN POINT)

(The **Deliverance** story from Exodus)

(Another easy PEN POINT. Maybe the next one will be a bit more challenging.)

Can you find the hidden PEN POINT in chapter 10?

Chapter 10
Mrs. Willowkins to the Rescue

No sooner had the humans left the porch, than Daniel Coon climbed up the handrail and onto Mrs. Willowkins' bird feeder. Mr. Greenleaf made himself invisible inside the watering pot the 15 minutes the old scavenger ate his fill of cracked corn and black oil sunflower seeds. After his adversary vanished, the froggy hopped out to enjoy the magnificent, midsummer night.

Sparkling stars in the night sky shimmered like tiny diamonds on black, velvet tapestry, and moonbeams hopscotched on Blue Heron Lake to the merry tune of the cricket choir. Mr. Greenleaf felt exceptionally merry himself and sang,

"The Lord is good to me,

And so I thank the Lord,

For giving me the things I need..."

"Hmmm," he said. "What does a froggy need? Ah-ha! I think I've got it!

A home and a friend and a bug to eat,

The Lord is good to me."

In one and a half jumps, Mr. Greenleaf plopped beside the screen wall separating tree frog and Fern.

"Good evening, dear Fern," said Mr. Greenleaf. "You must hear my latest discovery from the fascinating Bible story Mrs. Willowkins told the wee-humans tonight - who, by the way, are faithful wee-friends and not predators after all."

Fern stared in disbelief.

"It's entirely true!" insisted Mr. Greenleaf. "Today, the wee one, called Jacob, courageously rescued me from imprisonment inside the big house over Blue Heron Lake and carried me ever so gingerly

in his wee hands back to my watering pot atop Big-Blue Mountain. Nevertheless, as I was saying, these Bible stories are simply mesmerizing; and tonight, I learned that not only is the Lord our God, but the Lord is also our *Guide*. The Lord made everything and never for an instant intended His handiwork to just scape by – struggling the best we can in our own efforts while living on this ole earth. His intention, on the contrary, has forever been to guide and take care of His animal-creatures, as well as the he, she, and wee-humans. Therefore, I have concluded that across this unforgettable summer, when Cousin Kelly Greenleaf, the fireflies, Barnabas Fieldmouse, Orville McNutt, Mrs. Willowkins, and little Jacob came to my aid, in actuality, it was the Lord God Himself helping and guiding Jumping Jehoshaphat Greenleaf."

The next day, while Mr. Greenleaf slept contently in the hollow handle of his watering pot atop Big-Blue Mountain, the adult-child-humans packed their suitcases and then loaded luggage, toys, grandchildren, and granddog, Lucy, into the gray minivan to go visit the other Alabama grandparents.

"We didn't get to tell Mr. Green Jeans goodbye," cried Isaac.

"It's daytime now, dear," said Mrs. Willowkins. "Mr. Green Jeans is fast asleep. Remember? I'll tell him bye for you the next time I see him. I promise."

Mr. and Mrs. Willowkins blew kisses and waved until the van disappeared from sight. When Mr. Williowkins noticed tears trickling down his bride's normally happy face, he put his arm around her small shoulders and tenderly kissed her forehead.

"We'll see them again soon, sweetie pie. Before you know it, we'll be heading north to celebrate Jacob's birthday. You know what they say - time flies when your having fun - and we find the fun in each new day," said Mr. Willowkins encouragingly.

She smiled.

Mrs. Willowkins decided to use a different watering pot for the remainder of the summer so as not to disturb her little frog friend. Following the grandchildren's departure, however, weeks passed from July to August to September, and Mrs. Willowkins didn't see Mr. Greenleaf a single time.

"I wonder what's become of Mr. Green Jeans?" said Mrs. Willowkins.

"Maybe he grew tired of *someone* constantly moving his house and filling it with water and found another place to live," said Mr. Willowkins.

One mid-September afternoon, assuming Mr. Greenleaf had indeed moved, Mrs. Willowkins carried the watering pot from the high deck to an outdoor faucet by the driveway.

"Are you in there Mr. Green Jeans?" called Mrs. Willowkins.

Peering inside and seeing nothing, she filled the pot and toted it to the mailbox at the bottom of the steep hill. But the moment she began watering the fall mums, out hopped none other than Mr. Greenleaf himself.

"Mr. Green Jeans!" she cried. "Oh, my, Mr. Green Jeans, you'll never find your way back home from down here."

Quickly emptying the water onto the flowers, the she-human tried to coax the little, green tree frog back into the pot.

"Come on Mr. Green Jeans," pleaded Mrs. Willowkins, "jump in, and I'll take you back home."

"Where am I?" croaked Mr. Greenleaf who had completely slept through his she-human friend flooding his home and transporting froggy and pot to the bottom of the steep hill.

"Jump!" urged Mrs. Willowkins, but when she put the watering pot next to the frog, he leaped to the mailbox post instead. Mrs. Willowkins held the watering pot beside the post and gently touch his soft, green back. Mr. Greenleaf leaped again and this time, fortunately, stuck to the side of the pot.

"Hold on, Mr. Green Jeans!" said Mrs. Willowkins, and she jogged up the steep hill like a young schoolgirl in a foot race.

Unbeknownst to Mr. Greenleaf, the shortest trail back to Big-Blue Mountain was along the stone path beside the little goldfish pond in Mrs. Willowkins flower garden where Mr. Greenleaf had lived all his born days before Caiaphas Croaker's June invasion. Mrs. Willowkins knew a large bullfrog now lived in the fishpond; therefore, she sped by his territory and hollered, "Don't jump off now, Mr. Green Jeans! That big ole bullfrog will gobble you up in a Sasquatch second. Please, help me get this froggy home, Lord Jesus."

54

REFLECTIONS
POINTS to PONDER

1. Mrs. Willowkins accidentally carried Mr. Greenleaf all

   the way down the steep hill to the _____.

2. Mrs. Willowkins asked the Lord _____

   to help get Mr. Greenleaf home.

God's PROMISE to you:

"Jesus…will save His people from their sins." (Matt. 1:21)

(Hidden PEN POINT)

(**Jesus**, the Christ, the beloved Son of Father God, and the

Lord in whom we have blessing, grace, and the forgiveness

of our sins.)

(Read Ephesians 1:1-7)

Can you find the last hidden PEN POINT in chapter 11?

Chapter 11
Good News

Lickety-split and stone by stone, the she-human retraced Mr. Greenleaf's astonishing two-night journey from fishpond to mountaintop in less than two minutes. On the high deck, she lovingly set the watering pot in its rightful place beside the cobalt blue planter.

"Now, all is well, Mr. Green Jeans, and you're safe and sound once more," said Mrs. Willowkins. Looking upward to an autumn sky as blue as robin eggs, she added, "Thank You, Lord Jesus!"

Mrs. Willowkins walked inside the big house over Blue Heron Lake, and Mr. Greenleaf hopped behind the cobalt blue planter to catch his breath and calm his shaky, slim, lime legs.

"Fern," said Mr. Greenleaf, "you won't believe what just happened. I've unquestionably survived yet another hair-raising adventure with Mrs. Willowkins. Not that I have hair to raise, mind you. But if I did, I'm quite certain it would be sticking straight up like the black plume of a mountain quail - although the quail's plume is most indubitably a feather and not hair. Nonetheless, I tell you truthfully that I've weathered another spine-tingling ordeal! A torrent of water washed me from the handle hollow onto foreign soil. Instantly, the brave she-human wheedled me back onto the watering pot, and then she rapidly carted me up a steep incline, past the Croaker-infested fishpond, and up Big-Blue

Mountain; and I dare say, faster than a wild cheetah in the grasslands of Africa!"

Fern stood completely dumbfounded.

"Mrs. Willowkins talked to the Lord throughout the entire mission," said Mr. Greenleaf. "However, this time, she called Him by a special name – Jesus. And when she had me to safe haven, Mrs. Willowkins said as plain as day, 'Thank You, Lord Jesus.' I believe that's the most beautiful name I've ever heard – Jesus. What a remarkable day at the end of this unforgettable summer. The Lord is God, and He made everything. The Lord is my Guide, and His name is Jesus!"

That evening, Mr. and Mrs. Willowkins sat on the screen porch in the darkness, holding hands, and listened to God's wildlife menagerie surrounding Blue Heron Lake: bullfrog croaks, cricket twitters, whip-poor-will calls, and Sir Solomon's occasional who-who-ha-who. Mr. Greenleaf, on the other hand, listened attentively to the he and she humans' captivating conversation, which was momentarily interrupted by a ringing cell phone.

"Wilbur, it's the children," said Mrs. Willowkins cheerfully. "Hello."

After a pause, she said, "Oh, that's wonderful news, dear!"

"What'd they say?" said Mr. Willowkins.

"Let me put you on speakerphone so Papaw can hear, too," said Mrs. Willowkins.

"Hi, Papaw," said Elizabeth.

"Hi, sugar," said Mr. Willowkins. "What's all the excitement about?"

"I'm going to be baptized!" said Elizabeth.

Mr. Willowkins beamed and said, "So tell me, Elizabeth, why do you want to be baptized?"

"Because I believe Jesus is God's Son. I trust that He died on a cross for my sins and rose again. I love Him, and I want to follow Jesus all my life," said Elizabeth.

"That's such good news!" said Mr. Willowkins.

"We're so proud of you, dear," said Mrs. Willowkins. "When's the baptism?"

"A week from Sunday," said Elizabeth. "Can you come?"

"Of course!" Mr. and Mrs. Willowkins said at the same time.

"Lord willin' and the creek don't rise," said Mrs. Willowkins, "we'll be there, dear."

Long after the old couple retired for the night, Mr. Greenleaf sat under the star-spangled canopy and wondered and pondered and contemplated and mused and considered and thought and thought and thought about Elizabeth's good news.

"Even though I have much to learn about the Lord Jesus, I believe He is the Lord who loves me and takes care of me. I truly love Him, too, and want to follow Him all the days of my life, as well," said Mr. Greenleaf to Fern, his little, stone turtle friend.

At the end of his declaration, Mr. Greenleaf heard a peep. His teensy, green ears perked up as tall as teensy, green ears will perk, and he listened as hard as a little, green tree frog can listen. The peep sounded again, followed by another peep, and then another. Each peep became louder than the former until the peeping changed to audible words.

"Jumping Jehoshaphaaaat! Are you up here?" called a recognizable voice.

"I'm here!" cried Mr. Greenleaf. "I'm here! I'm here! I'm here!"

Mr. Greenleaf jumped from behind the cobalt blue planter, hopped toward that small voice bounding up the staircase, and landed nose to nose with Cousin Kelly Greenleaf on the top step of Big-Blue Mountain.

"You're alive!" said Mr. Greenleaf.

"As are you!" said Kelly.

"How did you escape Caiaphas Croaker? And how did you *ever* find me?" said Mr. Greenleaf.

"A kind Mr. Barnabas Fieldmouse encouraged me to search for you atop Big-Blue Mountain, and I've come bearing good news. Croaker is gone, vanished, extinct! Rumor has it that the ambush predator ventured down the hill in broad daylight to the big lake below our small fishpond and hopped too close to a Great Blue Heron. One gulp and that villain bullfrog was a goner forevermore."

"Oh, my," said Mr. Greenleaf.

"So, I tidied up your tiny cave myself and set out immediately to find you. Your pleasant cottage just one stone south and two rocks west of the waterfall is ready and waiting for you to return home where you belong."

Following Mr. Greenleaf's tearful goodbye to Fern, the Greenleaf cousins jumped down Big-Blue Mountain by way of the 15-step staircase, hopped across the cool concrete slab under the high screen porch, and then followed the stone pathway to the small goldfish pond in Mrs. Willowkins' lovely flower garden. That night, the cricket choir sang a spirited tune to the beat of bullfrog bellows rising from the big lake below, and Mr. Man-in-the-Moon smiled his frozen smile above the treetops. J. Jehoshaphat Greenleaf was home.

The froggy gazed at the starry heavens with his little, black peepers. "Thank You, Lord Jesus," said Mr. Greenleaf. "Cousin Kelly, I have some fabulous Good News to tell you!"

REFLECTIONS
POINTS to PONDER

1. What was Elizabeth's good news? She was going to be

   _____.

2. What Good News do you think Mr. Greenleaf told

   Kelly? I think he told Kelly the Good News of the

   Lord_____, our God and our Guide.

God's PROMISE to you:

"For this is how much God loved the world: He gave His

one and only Son [Jesus] so that everyone who believes in

Him will not perish but have eternal life."

(John 3:16 NLT)

(Hidden PEN POINT)

(The **Good News** of forgiveness of sins and everlasting

life through faith and trust in God's Son, Jesus Christ; and

that, dear friends, is the Gospel.)

(Read 1 Cor. 15:1-4)

AFTERWORD

Thank you for reading *Mr. Greenleaf's Unforgettable Summer*. Much of this story is make-believe, of course; however, the remainder is undeniably true!

- In the summer of 2014, I "met" Mr. Greenleaf when I brought my watering pot into my pink and green laundry room and filled it with water. The little, green tree frog lived in my pot on our high deck that entire summer.
- Also, a large bullfrog lived in our small, goldfish pond that same summer; and Fern, the stone turtle, still sits on our screen porch.
- Mr. Glassco and I have three married children, four grandchildren: Easton *Jacob*, Anya *Elizabeth*, Fisher *Isaac*, and Colton *Alexander*, and two granddogs: Gabe and Lucy.
- Easton really chased Mr. Greenleaf around my kitchen and carried him back outside, and Anya was indeed baptized later that summer.
- That September, I accidentally toted Mr. Greenleaf (hidden in the hollow handle of my watering pot) to the mailbox at the bottom of our hill, coaxed him back onto the pot after he jumped out, and speed-walked the froggy back to our high deck overlooking Blue Heron Lake.
- Most importantly, the Bible stories, PEN POINTS, and Gospel are absolutely true – God truly sent His Son, Jesus, to earth. Jesus lived, died on a cross, and rose to life again so that whosoever believes in Him will have never-ending, happily-ever-after life in heaven with God. Do *you* believe in Jesus? I do!!!

Jill Glassco

Made in the USA
Middletown, DE
23 April 2015